In memory of my Mukul (Aunty) Marika

About the Indigenous Literacy Foundation

The Indigenous Literacy Foundation (ILF) is a national charity working with Aboriginal and Torres Strait Islander remote Communities across Australia. We are Community-led, responding to requests from remote Communities for culturally relevant books, including early learning board books, resources, and programs to support Communities to create and publish their stories in languages of their choice.

In 2024 the ILF won the Astrid Lindgren Memorial Award, given annually to a person or organisation for their outstanding contribution to kids' or young adult literature.

First published in 2025 by the Indigenous Literacy Foundation
Gadigal Country
Level 17/207 Kent Street
Sydney NSW 2000
ilf.org.au

Cataloguing-in-Publication details are available
from the National Library of Australia

www.trove.nla.gov.au

ISBN 9781922592682

Typesetting and design by Lee Burgemeestre
Printed in China by RR Donnelley Asia Printing Solutions Limited

Thanks to ARDS Aboriginal Corporation
for translation and logistics support with this project.

On the way to Yalaŋbara

Written by Rärriwuy Gurramu Marika
Illustrated by Merrkiyawuy Ganambarr-Stubbs

INDIGENOUS LITERACY FOUNDATION

Yalmay and I were taking Jill
to our homeland, Yalaŋbara,
where the Djan'kawu sisters arrived
and created the Yolŋu people.
We had my father's sister and her
great-grandkids with us.

Jill had a car, and we had water
and the other things we needed.
She said it was a four-wheel drive,
but when they came to pick me up
I took one look and shook my head.

"I'm telling you now, that car won't make it."

About ten metres after we hit the sand, we got bogged.
Maybe Jill didn't turn the hubs on to four-wheel drive, maybe she did.
Either way, that car was good for gravel,
but not for getting us where we wanted to go.

We tried reversing, but the tyres began to spin.
We were going down, down into the sand.
We needed to dig. We started with our hands.

"Let's try again. Jump in, Jill."

Forward, reverse. "YES!! STOP."
But NO, the tyres of the car kept sinking into the sand.

Meanwhile, the sun was going up – higher and higher in the sky.
The sand was heating up. We were heating up.
Everything felt hot. Too hot for all this work.

We needed to sit in the shade and cool off.
We needed to lay down the mats,
have a cuppa tea, make some damper,
pull our shirts up and feel some breeze.

It was the build-up.
While we were sitting there,
I imagined the beach at Yalaŋbara,
the turquoise water and the milk
oysters that would be ready to eat.

We could be there, under the casuarina
trees or the coconut trees that my father,
the Old Man, planted back in the 1980s.

We could be swimming in the clear water
or fishing with our hand reels from the rocks,
catching red emperor, mangrove jacks,
coral trout and trevally.

We could be digging up
ghost crabs on the beach for bait.

We could be picking up shells as we walked,
and later making a tiny hole and threading them
onto fishing line for a necklace.

We could be seeing the small white morning glory flowers
that you don't find anywhere else.

We could be looking for a feed of turtle eggs,
following their tracks to find a low mound.

Turtle eggs look like ping pong balls. We collect them
for all the family – maybe one hundred eggs to share.

We use a casuarina stick with a pointy end and prod, prod, prod
until the stick sinks in soft sand. Then we dig.
It's a good reason to dig – digging for little white treasures.

The Old People pinch the rubbery shell and squirt them into their mouths
and eat them just like that. We prefer to cook them – boiled up or baked in
hot sand. They still stay runny – soft, salty and delicious.

But we were still sitting in the bush where we got bogged with the car.
And we weren't eating turtle eggs!

We could be eating mud crab.
We spear them and roast them on the fire.
They make good eating, those ones.
Mud crabs are as big as saucers.

There are lots of mudcrabs in the mangroves.
And mud mussels.
And crocodiles. We keep a lookout for them.

We could be sitting on the beach,
looking at the sea,
feeling that place healing us, calming us.

Anyone whether they're Yolŋu or balanda can feel the spirit of that place.
The Traditional Owners call out to the spirit of the Old People
so that they care for you. Country cares for you.
At Yalaŋbara you feel calmness in yourself. You feel relaxed.
At Yalaŋbara you are somebody.

While we're sitting there, I think of the time when my father and his father's two brothers and Dema Ŋurruwutthun went to Yalaŋbara in the 1970s.

Before that, no women or children could go to that place, but he could see into the future and the invasion of another culture. A few years later my father took us there.

Our Elders had to fight to protect that place. Sometimes people from outside want things they can't have.

Back then my father built a tin shack for us to live in. There was a pump for water, and the land and the sea for food. Everything we needed. That old shack has fallen down now, but we can still dig for fresh water in the sand.

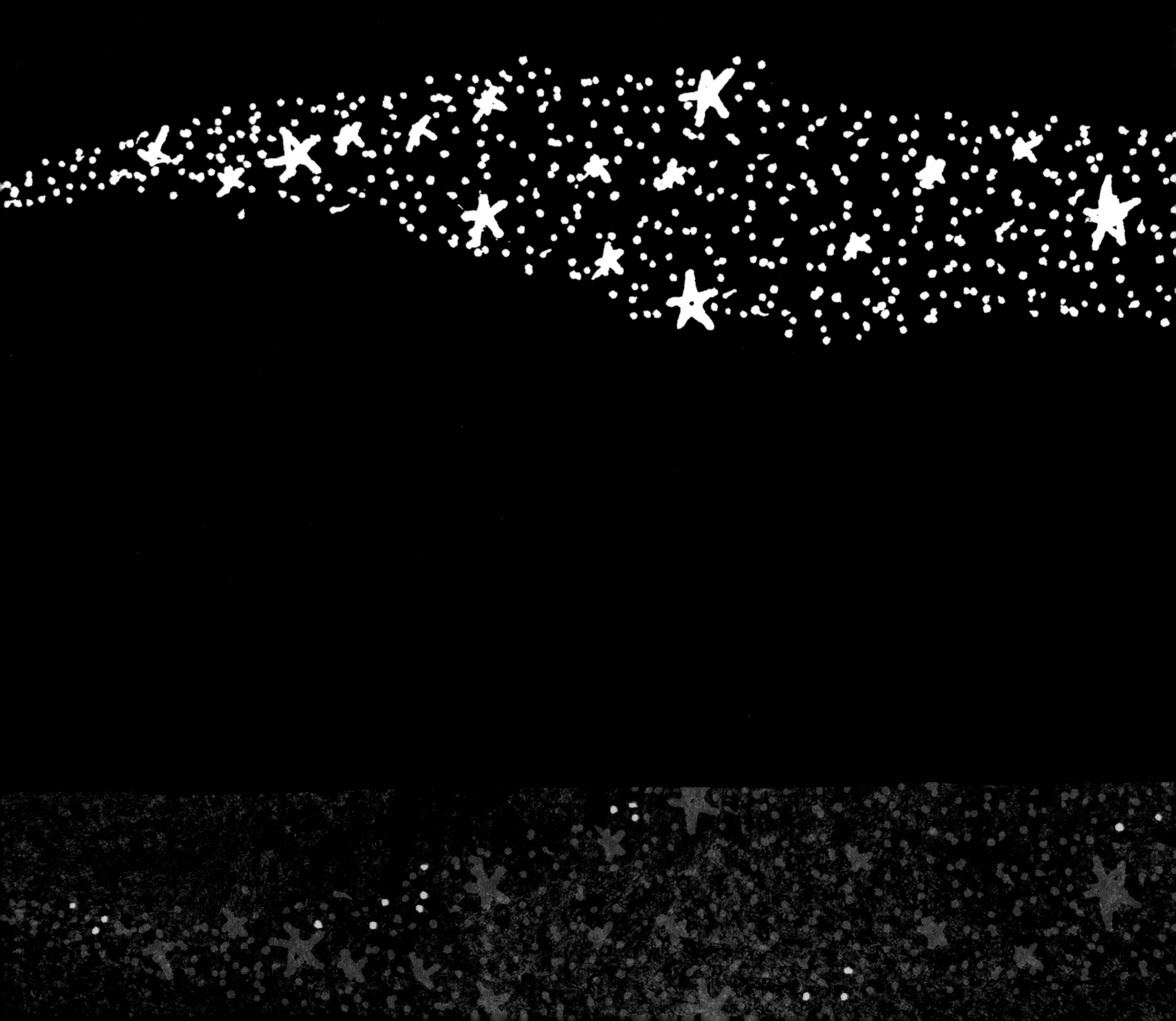

At night at Yalaŋbara we see the Milky Way.
We see the Southern Cross twinkling at us.
We see the moon's reflection on the dark sea.

We hear the surf crashing on the sand, and the sound of the wind.

We build a big fire and tell big stories. And little ones too. If it's windy we get some old tin to make a wind break and we listen.

All the stories – funny ones, sad ones, sometimes a romance, sometimes an adventure.

In the distance we see lights of fishing trawlers in the waters of the Gulf. We don't know where they come from – maybe on the currents flowing down from Macassar just like in the old days.

My mind goes to those Macassans.
To the stories of them coming to our shores, trading with the Old People.
They came for trepang (sea cucumbers) and mother-of-pearl.
They brought fishing hooks, calico, knives and machetes, tamarind trees and some words that are now part of our language. Those things are still with us today.

That's where we could have been, but we were not at Yalaŋbara.
We were on the mat, in the shade, looking at that car.

Yalmay called to us, "Damper's ready."
She jolted us back to sad, hot reality.

We ate and yarned and waited for the sun to go down until it was cooler. We rested and gathered our strength and then we dug again.

This time we gathered sticks, grass and twigs to push under the wheels and when Jill reversed, it worked!

A big cheer went up – **WE WERE OUT!**

Thinking about Yalaŋbara
makes me feel happy inside,
although I'm sad for not being there.
That day we didn't get there,
but we shared the shade and the stories
and the damper and the adventure.

Next time we will share the fish
and turtle eggs too.